QUE

THE

Due fo

A CERTAIN SLANT OF SUNLIGHT

TED BERRIGAN

O Books

INTRODUCTORY NOTE

Here's how these poems were written. Ken & Ann Mikolowski, the Alternative Press, sent Ted 500 blank postcards, to write on or do something to, whatever he wanted, each one individually. The postcards would later each be put in a packet of Alternative Press materials & sent out by the Mikolowskis to their subscribers. The blank postcards Ted used were 4½ × 7", in a sort of buff color.

Early on in the project Ted discovered he was writing a book of poems. He announced this fact to me, from time to time, & sometimes characterized the projected book as a book of postcard-like messages, sometimes as a book of short, or shorter, poems. Neither of these characterizations is particularly apt for what happened: a realm of shorter poems, written in a newly freed voice, that drifts among day-book, epigram & lyric, in all literary awareness, describing the feel of a difficult year. This was the year in which his mother died, & the year before he died; but any year might be a year of deaths—& there is always plenty of life in the midst of all this dying, isn't there? The idea of having the poems cover a year's time evolved from the fact that he received them at the beginning of 1982; he dated most of the poems, though he didn't intend for the dates to be printed—they were for his purposes, to help him shape the final book.

The working method tended to be to begin with something by someone else. Ted would give 4 or 5 postcards to someone & ask them to write a line or a few words on them—sometimes that person would take the cards home for a while, sometimes write on them right then in Ted's room. Or Ted would ask artist friends to do something to a few—draw, paint, paste something on. Or he would paste something on & then begin to doodle. Sometimes he would start with lines from someone else's poem or song. Occasionally he would write a poem he'd already written. A postcard might be subject to endless tinkering, the beauty of working on a 4½ × 7″ piece of stiff card being that you can always hold the card in your hand & do something else to it & keep having it right there in front of you, compact! and do some more to it & more & more. It's a very graspable, manageable unit.

Ted died six months after the last of these poems was completed & before he could select & order the poems into their book. He did give me some instructions, however, on how the book should be made. The title, horoscope, dedication, & first three poems are according to his instructions. Likewise that the title poem be somewhere near the beginning, possibly fourth. He asked that the dates be removed. He kept the poems, of which there are altogether about 160 (there may be more out in the world), in two folders; he told me which folder contained most of the poems he liked best. I further remembered from our conversations that he was hoping for a book of about a hundred poems. Keeping all this in mind, & loosely observing the chronology of the poems (I know he would not have strictly kept to it), I have made a selection of 100 poems (accidentally — I wasn't aiming precisely for that number) & tried to order them into a good read.

Ted also asked that the names of his "collaborators" not be printed on the page — to preserve a unity of voice throughout (& besides he did write most of the words), so I would like to acknowledge them here. They include Allen Ginsberg, Steve Carey, Greg Masters, Joanne Kyger, Steve Levine, Tom Pickard, Jeff Wright, Eileen Myles, Anne Waldman, & myself. My apologies to anyone I've omitted. Of artists who made pictures on the postcards, I remember George Schneeman, Dick Jerome, & Rosemary Mayer. Thanks. And I would also like to thank Ron Padgett (for advice).

ALICE NOTLEY
Dec. 18, 1987

A Certain Slant of Sunlight

Ted Berrigan

Poems

(13 Feb '82 ~ 31 July '82)
13 Feb 82 ~ 31 Dec 82

Edited by Alice Notley

for Tom Carey

POEM

Yea, though I walk
through the Valley of
the Shadow of Death, I
Shall fear no evil——
for I am a lot more
insane than
This Valley.

*

You'll do good if you play it like you're

       not getting paid.

But you'll do it better if the motherfuckers pay you.

(Motto of THE WHORES
& POETS GUILD — trans.
from The Palatine Anth-
ology by Alice Notley &
Ted Berrigan. 20 Feb 82)

)

*

With
daring
and
strength
men
like
Pollock,
de Kooning,
Tobey,
Rothko,
Smith
and
Kline
filled
their
work
with
the
drama,
anger,
pain,
and
confusion
of
contemporary
life.

Just
like
me.

A CERTAIN SLANT OF SUNLIGHT

In Africa the wine is cheap, and it is
on St. Mark's Place too, beneath a white moon.
I'll go there tomorrow, dark bulk hooded
against what is hurled down at me in my no hat
which is weather: the tall pretty girl in the print dress
under the fur collar of her cloth coat will be standing
by the wire fence where the wild flowers grow not too tall
her eyes will be deep brown and her hair styled 1941 American
      will be too; but
I'll be shattered by then
But now I'm not and can also picture white clouds
impossibly high in blue sky over small boy heartbroken
to be dressed in black knickers, black coat, white shirt,
      buster-brown collar, flowing black bow-tie
her hand lightly fallen on his shoulder, faded sunlight falling
across the picture, mother & son, 33 & 7, First Communion Day, 1941 —
I'll go out for a drink with one of my demons tonight
they are dry in Colorado 1980 spring snow.

BLUE GALAHAD

for Jim Carroll

Beauty, I wasn't born
High enough for you :   Truth
I served ; her knight :   Love
In a Cold Climate.

SALUTATION

"Listen, you cheap little liar . . . "

THE EINSTEIN INTERSECTION

This distinguished boat
Now for oblivion, at sea, a
Sweet & horrid joke in dubious taste,
That once, a Super-Ego of strength, did both haunt
Your dreams and also save you much bother, brought
You to The American Shore ; Out of The Dead City carried you,
Free, Awake, in Fever and in Sleep, to the
City of A Thousand Suns where, there, in the innocent heart's
Cry & the Mechanized Roar of one's very own this, The 20th
      Century, one's
Own betrayed momentary, fragmented Beauty got
Forgotten, one Snowy Evening, Near a Woods, because
The Horse Knows the Way ; because of, "The Hat on the Bed," and
Because of having "Entered the Labyrinth, finding No Exit.", is
That self-same ship, the "U.S.S. Nature" by name, that D.H. Lawrence
      wrote one of his very best poems about ;
THE SHIP OF DEATH. (a/k/a THE CAT CAME BACK) !

PINSK AFTER DARK

Reborn a rabbi in Pinsk, reincarnated
        backward time,
I gasped thru my beard full of mushroom barley
        soup;
two rough-faced blonde Cossacks, drinking
        wine,
paid me no heed, not remembering their futures —
        Verlaine, & Rimbaud.

REDS

There isn't much to say to Marxists in Nicaragua
        with .45's
afraid of the U.S. Secretary of State, eating
        celery.
Back in New York, "we saw a beautiful movie,"
        Allen said.   "It made me cry."
"I hadda loan him my big green handkerchief, so
        he could blow his nose!" Peter Orlovsky laughed.

PEOPLE WHO CHANGE THEIR NAMES

Abraham & Sarah.

Naomi — ("Call me not Naomi,
    call me Mara; for The Almighty
      hath dealt very bitterly with me.")

Simon, who shall be called Peter.

St. Paul (formerly Saul).

Joseph of Arimathea.

Cain.

Libby Notley ("when I was six I found out my
      real name was Alice");

Francis Russell O'Hara; Didi Susan Dubleyew;
Ron Padgett; Dick Gallup;

STEVE CAREY:

Kenneth Koch (formerly Jay Kenneth Koch):

Jackson Pollock; "Rene" Rilke; William Carlos
Williams;

    my mother, Peg;

        Guillaume Apollinaire;

"Joe" Liebling: John Kerouac: Joe Howard
Brainard: "Babe Ruth":

Tom Clark; Anselm Hollo; Clark Coolidge;

    George & Katie Schneeman.

Samuel R. "Chip" Delaney.

IN THE LAND OF PYGMIES & GIANTS

Anselm! Edmund!
    Get me an ashtray!
No one in this house
In any way is any longer sick!
        And I am the Lord, and owner
           of their faces.
        They call me, Dad!

ANGST

I had angst.

CAESAR

Caesar,
I could care less
whether your Grandma
was black,
or white —
you'll always be a nigger to me.

Gaius Valerius Catullus
(trans. Ted Berrigan)

"POETS TRIBUTE TO PHILIP GUSTON"

I hear walking in my legs
Aborigines in the pipes
I am the man your father was
Innocence bleats at my last
Black breaths — and tho I was considered a royal
        pain in the ass by
Shakespeare's father, the high alderman,
All the deadly virtuous plague my death!
I could care less?

BLUE HERRING

fiction appears) for I and only one per-
son's eyes.   In my more iconoclastic
moments I stifle the impulse to send
such poems, which I do come across
them, back to their authors, taking
same authors to task for presuming
too much and asking them to send
their poem right on to the faceless
As if you hands were innocent
and the lobsters in your groin
And the heart of the scarecrow opens like snow
And something in the branches makes the pigeons
    spread their wings
You reach into the branches and grab the red herrings —
    the
Fountain of Youth is uncharted
You are its overflowing outline
You can only laugh.

JOY OF SHIPWRECKS

for Jeff Wright

Stoop where I sit, am crazy
in sunlight on, brown as stone,
like me, (stoned, not brown; I
am white, like writer trash), see
that stick figure, chalky, also
white, with tentative grin, walking
toward us? Feel your blood stirring?
That's Eileen, as typical as sunlight
in the morning; typical as the morning
the morning after a typical Eileen night

"EILEEN" (detail)

for George Schneeman

When she comes, landscape listens; heavenly
Winter afternoons; shadows hold their breath;
she is the seal on despair; affection; tunes
sent us of the air

None may teach her anything; weight;
despair; imperious death;
She is light; she is certain; she
is where the meanings are.

Going, even, she's impressive; like
internal distance; death; Myles
Where the meanings are; she sends us;
She is of and like the air; a star.

O CAPTAIN, MY COMMANDER, I THINK

I like First Avenue
when the time of the fearful trip is come
& the Lady is for burning, as the day's begun
to duck
          behind the Levy-Cohen Housing Project
whose sand-pond can be seen still, through binoculars,
by the First Tyrant-Mistress of The Near West;
sky falls; & night; & me, too, yr star:
When the lilacs come I'll flip
til thrice I hear your call, darkling thrush.

POLISH HAIKU

The Pope's learning Welsh :
> (he's an alien).
More power to him !

ODE

Spring banged me up a bit

      & bruised & ruddy &
      devastatingly attractive
      I made

2 A. M. Phone call to Bill Brown

      'How long is your foot?'
      'Oh about 12 inches.'
      'Well stick it up your Ass.'

         *

"and Day rang from pool to hilltop
             like a bell."

SUNNY, LIGHT WINDS

those exhausting dreams
of angry identification, a dog
like ego, Snowflakes as kisses — the
ability to forget is a sign of a
    happy mind — at least,
Philip thinks it is, & he's happy,
            sometimes.
But I don't *want* no cornbread &
            molasses!
Never. I don't *want* to live in the un-
    tidy
moment! Forget it. I don't want no
            lover
who always wants to be the boss!
Want! Want! Want! — it's all right, I'm
Just having a little fun, Mother.
unhappy love affairs,
are only for madmen

revery

WHAT A DUMP

or,

EASTER

(*for Katie Schneeman*)

a metal fragrant white
    Capitol of beantown
sans dome; rubber & metal pieces
    of Kentucky; chicken-bones &
Light Cavaliers; jeans; tops; balls; caps;

"Now I have to have life
    after dreams"

"& now I'm running running
    running
down the King's Highway"

"& now I am Lily, Rosemary, & the Jack
    of Hearts;
One-eyed Jill; Pietro Gigli; 2 cats:
Howard; & Katie, my heart; & mine"

"Mine is melancholy"

"Mine is ½ gristle, ½ dust"

"Mine is Luke Skywalker, & his parts:
the Wookie part; the Landro part; the Han dynasty;
C-3PO"

"Mine is this 'Squeeze-box';
the Good; the Beautiful; the True; & Bucky Dent.
He just *has to* have a chance to be in The Hall of Fame!"

All pleased rise
Cleansed
Pure
In perfect order go.

PACIOREK

for Anselm Hollo

Light takes the bat, &
shoulder; who can tell us
how? (I wake to sleep, &
take my waking fast). O low-
ly worm, falling down upstairs,
& down is a lowly thing, how
fast is no longer a joy?

9 :16 & 2 :44, & 25 MINUTES TO 5

Dear Management's beautiful daughters,
                              sweetly
made Marion, & Alice, the Elephant——,
                              the
trouble with you two is just happened for
the first time ever, which is once more than
I can hold my head up under ever after again—If
Anybody asks you who made up this song, just tell 'em
It was me, & I've done been here & gone.

MY LIFE & LOVE

for Phil Whalen

"Do you
think I'll
ever see
him again?

　　"Beauty
　whose action is
　no stronger than a
　　　　flower?

　"I think I'm about to be
　　　　surpassed again.

"Do you think we'd better go to
　　　　California?"

"Naw.　Don't be silly.　Send him a round
　　cheese or something.　A can
　　　　of peaches."

HELLO, SUNSHINE,

Take off your head; un-
loose the duck; lift up your
heart, and quack! I am the
Morning Glory, I take no
back talk. . . .

Take me twice each morning;

   be funny that way.

IN MORTON'S GRILLE

In Morton's Grille I
always get nostalgia for Morton's Grille
which wasn't called Morton's Grille
at all, but THE RIVIERA CAFE, way out on
Elmwood Avenue.   They had a machine,
this was before TV, you put a quarter in
& a zany 3 minute movie of the Hatfields
shooting at the McCoys out a log cabin
window came on ; the McCoy's ran out of
bullets, so they started singing, "Pass the
Biscuits, Mirandy !"   Grandma's biscuits were
so hard, terrible, but saved the day when thrown
at the real McCoys.

ST. MARK'S IN THE BOUWERIE

for Harris Schiff

Naked
with a lion
a small lesbian
smoking a pipe
some silent young men
"Shit!" they exclaim
"Fuck all women!"
They all start singing patriotic songs

DINNER AT GEORGE & KATIE SCHNEEMAN'S

She was pretty swacked by the time she
Put the spaghetti & meatballs into the orgy pasta
    bowl—There was mixed salt & pepper in the
"Tittie-tweak" pasta bowl—We drank some dago red
    from glazed girlie demi-tasse cups—after
which we engaged in heterosexual intercourse, mutual
    masturbation, fellatio, & cunnilingus.　For
dessert we stared at a cupboard full of art critic
    friends, sgraffitoed into underglazes on vases.　We did
have a very nice time.

LISTEN, OLD FRIEND

"This ability, to do things well,
and to do them with precision & with
modesty, is nothing but plain & simple
                                    Vanity.
"It is Pride overfertilizes the soil
till alone the blue rose, grow — I know

Dante Alighieri told me so."

                          (signed :)

                          THE SLOTH

DINOSAUR LOVE

for Anne & Reed

Anne Lesley Waldman says, No Fossil Fuels
The best of the free times are still yet to come
With all of our running & all of our coming if we
Couldn't laugh we'd both go insane — with changes
       of attitudes
At the Horse Latitudes — if we couldn't laugh, we'd
       All be insane —
but right here with you, the living seems true, &
the gods are not burning us just to keep warm.

SPELL

A sparrow whispers in my loins
Geranium plus Geronimo forever
Across the wide Missouri
We drive us.

FOR ROBT. CREELEY

"In My Green Age"
like they say,
            much compassion,
            little dismay,
                such exuberance—

Loving: *Caught:*   *Back:*

There's a place—
"tho are be were as now is now...."

FINE MOTHERS

With sound   Sun melts snow
    Elms fill in
and wind blows green. ("When the wind
was green"...)   This is the Spring I knew
               would come.
The rosy finches row through.

day moves   then, my room—   light-
nights   bat their yellow dust against
the windows, & I dream   I am black
running, rising, to the sea :

Evenings, night heroes stop here, or,
                   gently pass
The trees release   into sky.
               Travelling by,
from grove to Mars,
         SEVEN arc over.
I call them angels.   O, angels,
O, common & amazing.

PANDORA'S BOX, AN ODE

. . . was 30 when we met.   I was
21.   & yet he gave me the impression
he was vitally interested in what I
was doing & what was inside me!   One
was Tremendous Power over all friends.
Power to make them do whatever.   Wed.   Bed.
Dig the streets.   Two is speeding and pills
to beef up on on top of speeding ills.   Three,
assumptions.   Four, flattery.   Five, highly
articulate streets, & when he saw me I was witty.
I was good poetry.   Love was all I was.   As
the case is, he had or was a charm
of his own.   I had the unmistakable signature
of a mean spirit.   Very close to breaking in.
I was like Allen Ginsberg's face, Jack's face,
eye to eye on me.   Face of Allen.   Face of Kerouac.
It was all in California.   Now,
all of my kingdoms are here.

TO BOOK-KEEPERS

The Final Chapters
of the History
        of
Modernism are
going to be written
in blood.   Yours,
you poor Immigrants!

THE SCHOOL WINDOWS SONG

(after Vachel Lindsay)

High School windows are always broken ;
Somebody's always throwing rocks,
Somebody always throws a stone,
Playing ugly playing tricks.

Jr. High windows are always broken, too :
There are plenty of other windows that never
       get broken ;
No one's going into Midtown & throwing rocks
At & through big, Midtown, store-windows.

Even the Grade School windows are always
Broken : where the little kids go to school.
Something is already long past terribly wrong.
End of The Public-School Windows Song.

TRANSITION OF NOTHING NOTED AS FASCINATING

The Chinese ate their roots; it
made them puke. We don't know til
we see our own. You are irre-
sistible. It makes me blush. How you
see yourself is my politics. O Turkey,
Resonance in me that didn't even want to know
what it was, still there, don't ever make jokes
about reality in Berkeley, they don't
understand either one there.
Donald Allen, Donald Keene, Wm. "Ted" deBary,
it's hard to respect oneself,
but I would like to be free.
China Night. Cry of cuckoo. Chinese moon.

WHOA BACK BUCK & GEE BY LAND!

(for Wystan Auden, &
Thelonious Sphere Monk)

This night my soul, & yr soul, will be wrapped in
    the same dark shroud
While whole days go by and later their years ;
Sleep, Big Baby, sleep your fill
With those daimones of Earth, the Erinyes,
Women in the night who moan yr name.
"Man, that was Leadbelly !"

FRANCES

Now that I
With you
Since
Leaving
Each day seems
The night
Tired with
Languisht
Suffering
While you
Nor I
With that
I feel.

SWEET IRIS

Take these beads from my shoulders
There's your paintings on the walls
Turn around slow & slowly
Help me make it through the night
Then I'll take you out for breakfast
Never see you all my life

I DREAMT I SEE THREE LADIES IN A TREE

for Douglas Oliver, Denise
Riley, & Wendy Mulford

If someone doesn't help me soon I
believe I'm going to lose my mind, I
mean my tone of voice, my first clue
as to what this speaker is like.   Help! (he).

is a beautiful piece of work in that it
has to spill out & still stand as
meeting own requirements :   dedicated to Betty
Chapman of Coon, Minnesota :   take me deeper

via from the outside, you, my unforgettables, my
best.   Hand, 2 hands, wheel, & blood ; O broken-hearted
Mystery that used to sing to me :   now I'm too misty,
and too much in love.   O lovely line that doesn't give an
        inch, but gives.

MOAT TROUBLE

He was wounded, & so
    was having
    Moat Trouble.

HOLLYWOOD

paid Lillian Gish $800,000 to
disappear so lovely so pure like milk
seems but isn't because of the fall-out
but it would have only cost me five & didn't,
so I did, but when Garbo is the temptress
doesn't it seem absolutely perfect-
ly right? just being there? nothing
costs anything that's something, does it?
like soaking at a Rosenthal/Ceravolo Poetry Reading
or blazing while "The White Snake" unfolds
itself: in the city, there one feels free, while
in the country, Peace, it's wonderful, & worrisome
I've never seen a peaceful demonstration, have you?
NO MORE NUKES

LAST POEM

for Tom Pickard

I am the man yr father & Mum was
When you were just a wee insolent tyke
until at 5 o'clock in the afternoon
on one of the days of infamy, & there
were many, & more to come yet, the goons
& the scabs of Management set upon us
Jarrow boys, & left us broken, confused
and alone in the ensuing brouhaha.   They
outnumbered us 5 to 1; & each had club
knife or gun.   Kill them, kill them, my
sons.   Kill their sons.

MUTINY!

The Admirals brushed
the dandruff off their
epaulets and steamed
on the H.M.S. Hesper
toward Argentina.   I
like doggies on their "little
feet", don't you, I said, but
they kept rolling over, be-
neath the tracer bullets and
the Antarctic moon, beneath the
daunting missiles and the Prince
in his helicopter, they were
steaming toward interesting places,
to meet interesting people, and
kill them.   They were at sea,
and it was also beneath them.

JO-MAMA

The St. Mark's Poetry Project
is closed for the summer.   But
all over the world, poets
are writing poems.   Why?

MONTEZUMA'S REVENGE

In order to make friends with the natives
In my home town, I let them cut off my face
By the shores of Lake Butter, on
The 7th anniversary of their arrival
In our Utopia.   It was the First of May.
Nose-less, eye-less, speechless, and
With no ears, I understood their reasoning,
And will spend the rest of my days
helping them cover their asses.   Free.

TURK

for Erje Ayden

"There's no place
     to go
   my heart,
 for all your
   100,000
   words."

M'SIEUR & MADAME BUTTERFLY

I go on loving you
Like water   Yggdrasil
Where you are 100,000 flowers
bloom   while across the
broken eggshell field the ink
rises from the fossils, as my
tongue drifts lightly into the Gobi Desert of yr
ear   & we become a person's lungs & take to the air.

WANTONESSE

Heart of my heart
Fair, & enjoyable
Harmlessly spooky
Loving her back

CREATURE

for Alice Notley

Before I was alive
    I were a long, dark, continent
Lonely from the beginning of time
    Behind Midnight's screen on St. Mark's Place

And my thin, black, rage
    Did envelop my pale, dusty, willowy-green-
Shell in dark bricks & black concrete
    'til I was a Hell that was not fire, but only hot.

Then I called you to bring me
    One more drink, & your good legs
And translucent heart brought me
    A city, which I put on, & became
Glad, & I walked toward Marion's &
    Helena's, to be seen, & found beautiful,
And was, & I came alive, & I cried Love!

XIII

(after Jack Kerouac)

O Will Hubbard in the night! A great writer today he is,
he is a shadow hovering over Western Literature, and
no great writer ever lived without that soft and
tender curiosity, verging on maternal care, about what
others say & think, (think & say), no great writer
ever packed off from this scene on earth without
amazement like the amazement he felt because
I was myself.

PROVIDENCE

Lefty Cahir, loan me your football shoes again—
Clark, let me borrow the brown suit once more—
I hear a fluttering against my windows.
River, don't rise above the 3rd floor.

PARIS, FRANCES

I tried to put the coffee back together
For I knew I would not be able to raise the fine
Lady who sits wrapped in her amber shawl
Mrs. of everything that's mine right now, an interior
Noon smokes in its streets, as useless as
Mein host's London Fog, and black umbrella, & these pills
Is it Easter? Did we go? All around the purple heather?
Go fly! my dears. Go fly! I'm in the weather.

WINDSHIELD

There is no windshield.

STARS & STRIPES FOREVER

for Dick Jerome

How terrible a life is
And you're crazy all the time
Because the words don't fit
The heart isn't breakable
And it has a lot of dirt on it
The white stuff doesn't clean it & it can't
     be written on
Black doesn't go anywhere
Except away & there isn't any
Just a body very wet & chemistry
which can explode like salt & snow
& does so, often.

MINNESOTA

If I didn't feel so
bad, I'd feel so good!

I HEARD BREW MOORE SAY, ONE DAY

for Allen Ginsberg

Go in Manhattan,
Suffer Death's dream Armies in battle!
Wake me up naked:
Solomon's Temple The Pyramids & Sphinx sent me here!

The tent flapped happily spacious & didn't fall down —
Mts. rising over the white lake 6 a.m. — mist drifting
          between water & sky —
Middle-aged & huge of frame, Martian, dim, nevertheless I
          flew from bunk
into shoe of brown & sock of blue, up into shining morning
          light, by suns,

landed, & walked outside me, & the bomb'd dropped
all over the Lower East Side!   What new element
Now borne in Nature?, I cried.   If I had heart attack now
Am I ready to face my mother?   What do?   Whither go?
How choose now?, I cried.   And, Go in Manhattan, Brew Moore
                                        replied.

POSTCARD

THE SENDER OF THIS
POSTCARD IS SECRETLY
(STILL) UNSURE OF YOUR WORTH
AS (EITHER) A FRIEND OR A
HUMAN BEING.   YOU COCKSUCKER.

SMASHED ASHCAN LID

for George Schneeman

Oh, George — that
utter arrogance! So
that people can't tell that
you're any good —

"chases dirt", for Chrissakes!!

OKAY. FIRST. . . .

"Truth is that which,
Being so, does do its
work."
(I said That.)

July 11, 1982

Dear Alice,

        The reason I love
you so much is be-
cause you're very
beautiful & kind.   I
also appreciate your
intelligence, though what
"intelligence" is I'm not
sure, & your wit, which
resembles nothing I've
ever thought about.

        Your loving husband,

        Ted Berrigan

THE WAY IT WAS IN WHEELING

(after Freddy Fender)

I met her in The Stone Age,
    riding shotgun — I can
Still recall that neon sign she
    wore — She was
Cramlin' through the prairie near
    the off-ramp, & I
Knew that she was rotten to the core.

I screamed, in pain, I'd live off her
    forever — She
Sd to me, she'd have a ham-on-
    rye — but who'd have
Thought she'd yodel, while in labor?
    I never had a chance
To say Good-bye!

MY AUTOBIOGRAPHY

For love of Megan I danced all night,
fell down, and broke my leg in two places.
I didn't want to go to the doctor.
Felt like a goddam fool, that's why.
But Megan got on the phone, called
my mother.   Told her, Dick's broken
his leg, & he won't go to the doctor!
Put him on the phone, said my mother.
Dickie, she said, you get yourself
up to the doctor right this minute!
Awwww, Ma, I said.   All right, Ma.
Now I've got a cast on my leg from
hip to toe, and I lie in bed all day
and think.   God, how I love that girl!

DOWN ON MISSION

There is a shoulder in New York City
Lined, perfectly relaxed, quoted really, quite high
Only in the picture by virtue of getting in
to hear Allen Ginsberg read, 1961
And though the game is over it's beginning lots of
        years ago,
And all your Cities of Angels, & San Francisco's are
        going to have to fall, & burn again.

IN YOUR FUCKING UTOPIAS

Let the heart of the young
        exile the heart of the old : Let the heart of the old
Stand exiled from the heart of the young : Let
        other people die : Let Death be inaugurated.
Let there be Plenty Money.   & Let the
Darktown Strutters pay their way in
To The Gandy-Dancers Ball.   But Woe unto you, O
        Ye Lawyers, because I'll be there, and
                I'll be there.

DICE RIDERS

Nothing stands between us
except Flying Tigers
Future Funk
The Avenue B Break Boys
    and
The Voidoids—
Sometimes,
Time gets in the way, &
sometimes, lots of sometimes,
We get in its way, so,
Love, love me, do.

THE HEADS OF THE TOWN

for Harris Schiff

They killed all the whales
now they're killing all the acorns
I'm almost the last Rhinoceros
I guess I'd better kill them.

TO BE SERIOUS

You will dream about me
All the months of your life.
You won't know whether
That means anything to me or not.
You will know that.
It's about time
You know something.

W/O SCRUPLE

(for Bernadette Mayer)

The wicked will tremble, the food will rejoice
When he & I grow young again
For an hour or two on
Second Avenue, at Tenth
About 35 days from now —

     Although that will not get it;
     And that will not be that.

GEORGE'S CORONATION ADDRESS

With Faith we shall be able . . .
There will be peace on earth . . .
      & Capricious day . . .
maybe we'll be there, or true.
Speed the day then.

TOUGH COOKIES

You took a wrong turn in
1938.   Don't worry about it.

The sun shines brightest when
the others are sleeping.

There is a Briss in your
immediate future.

Take heart.   Shakespeare was
probably an asshole too.

Your life is rare and precious
& it has no mud.   Stay with it.

You have strange friends, but
they are going to be strangers.

Everything is Maya, but
you will never know it.

Your gaiety is not cowardice,
but it may be hepatitis.

SKEATS AND THE INDUSTRIAL REVOLUTION

(DICK JEROME, 3/4 View)
ink on paper

God: perhaps, 'The being worshipped. To
whom sacrifice is offered. *Not* allied to
'good', (which is an adjective, not a
'being.' *Godwit:* a bird, or, more recently,
a 'twittering-machine'; (from the Anglo-Saxon,
God-wiht: just possibly meaning, 'worthy creature.'
Viz. Isle of Wight — Isle of Creatures. See, also,
Song, folk; Childe Ballad # 478 : "I've been
a creature for a thousand years.". . . .)

BESA

(to the Gods)

He is guardian to the small kitten.
He looks so determined.
He has a graceful hunch.
Light swirls around his crown,
     wispy, blondish, round.
Three shades of blue surround
     him — denim,
Doorway, sky.   His hands are up,
His eyes are in his head.   He's
     my brother, Jack ;
Kill him & I kill you.

NATCHEZ

for Rosina Kuhn

I stand by the window
In the top I bought to please you

As green rain falls across Chinatown
You are blissed out, wired, & taping,
      15 blocks uptown

When I am alone in the wet & the wind
Flutes of rain hire me

Boogie-Men drop in to inspire me

IN THE DEER PARK

for Tom Carey

"I know where I'm going
"& I know where I came from
"& I know who I love
"but the Dear knows who I'll marry. . . ."

I bought that
striped polo shirt,
long-sleeves, for 75 cents,
& wore it every minute, that year

I got a sunburn
on my face & hands
I hadn't noticed it.
But when someone pointed it out
I said it felt good.

I was over
a year in that
Park. Never did
feel in a hurry.
I was "in love."

TOMPKINS SQUARE PARK

All my friends in the
park speak Latin :　when
they see me coming, they
say, "Valium ?"

WARRIOR

for Jeff Wright

I watch the road :   I am a line-
   man for the County.   City streets
await me, under lustrous purple skies, purple
   light,
each night.   Manhattan is a needle
   in the wall.   While
it's true, the personal, insistent, instant-
   myth music cuts
a little close to the bone
& I have to get up early for work tomorrow, still
   there's
lots of quail in Verona, & I am
jubilant with horror
because I'm searching for pain underneath
another overload.
I hear you singing in the wires.

SPACE

is when you walk around a corner
& I see you see me across Second Avenue
You're dressed in identifiable white
over your jeans & I'm wearing Navy —
Jacob Riis is beams of sunlight as
I cross against the light & we inter-
cept at the Indian Candy Store.   The
Family has gone off to Parkersburg, W. Virginia
The Chrysler Building is making the Empire State
stand tall, & friendly it leans your way
There's appointments for everybody
They don't have to be kept, either.

DRESSES FOR ALICE

We are the dresses for Alice.
We go on, or off, for solace.

NEW YORK POST

for Michael Brownstein

Two cops cruise East 9th
between First and A.   Talk
about schedules, they're on
the Graveyard Shift : 11 to 7
in the morning.   They are definitely
not boring.   As they pass, I waver,
with my pepsis, two beers, & paper :
what am I doing here?
Shouldn't I be home, or them?
But I guess I'm on this case, too. . . .

LET NO WILLFUL FATE MISUNDERSTAND

When I see Birches, I think
of my father, and I can see him.
He had a pair of black shoes & a pair of
        brown shoes,
bought when he was young and prosperous.
"And he polished those shoes, too, Man!"
"Earth's the right place for Love,"
he used to say.   "It's no help,
but it's better than nothing."
We are flesh of our flesh,
O, blood of my blood; and we,
We have a Night Tie all our own; & all
day & all night it is dreaming, unaware
that for all its blood, Time is the Sand-
paper; that The Rock can be broken; that
Distance is like Treason.   Something
There is that doesn't love a wall: I
am that Something.

UNCONDITIONAL RELEASE AT 38

for Dick Gallup

like carrying a gun
like ringing a doorbell
like kidnapping Hitler
like just a little walk in the warm Italian sun . . .
like, "a piece of cake."
like a broken Magnavox
like the refrigerator on acid
like a rope bridge across the Amazon in the rain
like looking at her for a long few seconds
like going to the store for a newspaper
like a chair in a dingy waiting-room
like marriage
like bleak morning in a rented room in a pleasant, new city
like nothing else in the world now or ever

ASS-FACE

"This is the only language you understand, Ass-Face!"

MINUET

the bear eats honey

between the harbored sighs
inside my heart

where you were
no longer exists

blank bitch

BUENOS AIRES

Strings like stories shine
And past the window flakes of paper
Testimony to live valentine
A gracious start then hand to the chest
     in pain
And looking out that window.

MS. VILLONELLE

What is it all about—this endless
Talking & walking a night away—
Smoking—then sleeping half the day?
Typing a résumé, you say, smilingly.

THE WHO'S LAST TOUR

Who's gonna kiss your pretty little
    feet?

Who's gonna hold your hand?

Who's gonna kiss your red, ruby
    lips?

Who's gonna be your man, love,

    Who's gonna be yr

       man? Why,

I am. Don'tcha know? Why, I am.

TO SING THE SONG, THAT IS FANTASTIC

Christmas in July, or
Now in November in
        Montreal
Where the schools are closed,
& the cinnamon girls
        Sing in the sunshine
Just like Yellowman :
The soldiers shoot the old woman
        down
They shoot the girl-child on
        the ground : we
Steal & sell the M-16s, use
The money to buy the weed
The sky is blue & the Erie is
        Clean ;
Come to us with your M-16 :
Soldier, sailor, Policeman, Chief,
Your day is here & you have come
        to Grief.
Sing the songs, & smoke the weed ;
The children play & the wind is green.

INTERSTICES

"Above his head
changed"

And then one morning to waken perfect-faced
Before my life began
cold rosy dawn in New York City
call me Berrigan

Every day when the sun comes up
I live in the city of New York
Green TIDE behind ; pink against blue
Here I am at 8 :08 p.m. indefinable ample rhythmic frame

not asleep, I belong here, I was born, I'm amazed to be here
It is a human universe : & I interrupts yr privacy
Last night's congenial velvet sky left behind . . . kings . . . panties
My body heavy with poverty (starch) missing you mind clicks
       into gear

November. New York's lovely weather hurts my forehead
On the 15th day of November in the year of the motorcar
But, "old gods work" so   sleeping & waking   someone I
       love calls me
into the clear

BAD TIMING

Somethings gotta be done! I thought.

Rusty I was?

BANG!   ("I fell right down
                         on the floor.   Just like
                         Dave DeBusschere.")
Slept a few days.

I woke up; just as Red's voice
                    said, "She is
                    hurting, we
                 must DEFEND tons
      of indistinguishable tones."

                 I said, "This sense

there was a way, I met in the possible

O.K.

Under my roof.

Mars.   Autumn.   Bills (on the Bill
                         scene).

       BILL ME.

THIS GUY

He eats toenails.
Is rude, vain, cruel, gloomy.
He talks with bitter cryptic wit.
Is unclean.   "Is this some
    new kind
of meatball?". . . . sitting in
    a rowboat,
waiting for a bite . . . . has
just asked — with considerable
gravitas — if he might be
    allowed
to become one of my suitors.
And I said yes.

A CITY WINTER

My friends are crazy with grief
& sorrows — their children are born
and their morning lies broken —
& now it's afternoon.

GIVE THEM BACK, WHO NEVER WERE

I am lonesome after mine own kind — the
hussy Irish barmaid; the Yankee drunk who was once
a horsecart Dr.'s son, & who still is, for that matter;
The shining Catholic schoolboy face, in serious glasses,
with proper trim of hair, bent over a text by Peire Vidal,
& already you can see a rakish quality of intellect there;
Geraldine Weicker, who played Nurse in MY HEART'S IN
THE HIGHLANDS, on pills, & who eventually married whom? The
fat kid from Oregon, who grew up to be our only real poet;
& the jaunty Jamaica, Queens, stick-figure, ex US Navy, former
French Negro poet, to whom Frank O'Hara once wrote an Ode,
or meant to, before everything died, Fire Island, New
York, Summer, 1966.

VIA AIR

Honey,
      I wish you were here.
                  I wrote some poems about it.
And though it goes,
          and it's going,
               it will never leave us.

CHRISTMAS CARD

O little town of Bethlehem,
Merry Christmas
to Jim
& Rosemary.

CHRISTMAS CARD

for Barry & Carla

Take me, third factory of life!
But don't put me in the wrong guild.
So far my heart has borne even
the things I haven't described.

Never be born, never be died.

POEM

The Nature of the Commonwealth
the whole body of the People
flexed her toes and
breathed in pine.

I'm the one that's so
radical, 'cause all I do is pine.   Oh I just
can't think of anything —
No politics.   No music.   Nobody.   Nothing but sweet

Romance.   Per se.   De gustibus non disputandum est.
Flutters eyelashes.   Francis, my house is falling down.
Repair it.   Merry Christmas.

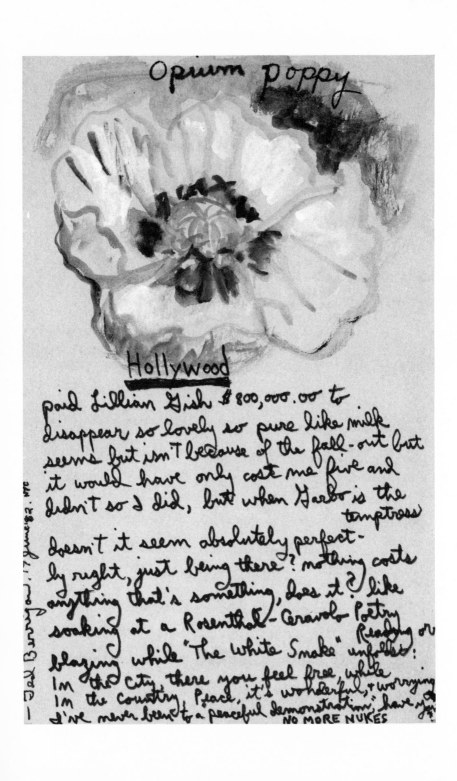

Opium poppy

Hollywood

paid Lillian Gish $800,000.00 to
disappear so lovely so pure like milk
seems but isn't because of the fall-out but
it would have only cost me five and
didn't so I did, but when Garbo is the
                                                    temptress
doesn't it seem absolutely perfect-
ly right, just being there? nothing costs
anything that's something, does it? like
soaking at a Rosenthal-Ceravolo Poetry
                                                    Reading or
blazing while "The White Snake" unfolds:
I'm in the city, there you feel free, while
I'm in the country, Peace, it's wonderful, & worrying
I've never been to a peaceful demonstration, have you
                                                    NO MORE NUKES

— Ted Berrigan, 17 June '82, NYC

EUREKA!

I left the bookstore stunned + giggling
between Baudelaire + Betjeman my books
in print took up nearly a foot. — I
walked several blocks to my car —
glowing at having reduced the competit;
not to mention John Ashbery + John
                                    Berryman;
after all, how many Johns does one poem
                                    need?,
to mere, forlorn, lonely manifestations
of the lame, the limp, the loud, and one
                                    Knight. —

got in, put it in reverse, and backed up
       a block and ½. I was home. Odd
having a car in Manhattan! Now home,
stretched out on the bed, I'm working on #233
of my next work, "500 American Postcards,
Now I've stopped, to do this one, # 13 today!
Oops! Wait a minute. Will this fit on a
       Postcard? J. Conrad, here I come

Love Poem

"I love Alice Notley," I
told Bill de Kooning, in
May of '82.

— Ted Berrigan
11 May 1982
NYC

SAN FRANCISCO

You took me
for everything
I have

I had it

Thanks
for that
you

~Ted Berrigan
17 June 79

Ronka

I'm gonna embarass
                    my mother
                +
I'm gonna embarass
                    my brother
                    +
    I'm gonna embarass
                    even my wife
but I'm not gonna embarass my life,
            O No,
I'm not gonna embarass my life,
                    not ever,
    I'm not gonna embarass my life,
    Not for you, or her, or anyone.
I'm never gonna embarass my life —
        except if I do . . .
        + if it does,
        Tough Shit.

(28 June '82)   - Ted Berrigan

ACKNOWLEDGMENTS:

Cover postcard by Ted Berrigan & George Schneeman, from the collection of Susan Cataldo.

The poem "Angst" first appeared in *In a Blue River,* by Ted Berrigan (Little Light Books, 1981). Also, many of these poems were originally published in poetry magazines; the editor cannot recall them all, but they must have included *Tangerine, Tamarind, The Poetry Project Newsletter, The World, Ahnoi, Little Light, Gandhabba, Bombay Gin, Friction,* & *New American Writing,* among others.

NOTE: In the poem "Blue Herring," "you hands" (line 9) is not a typo.

Other O Books

Phantom Anthems, Robert Grenier, 1986, $6.50
Dreaming Close By, Rick London, 1986, $5.00
Abjections: A Suite, Rick London, 1988, $3.50
Catenary Odes, Ted Pearson, 1987, $5.00
Visible Shivers, Tom Raworth, 1987, $8.00
O One/An Anthology, ed. Leslie Scalapino, 1988, $10.50

O Books
5729 Clover Drive
Oakland, CA 94618